SELECTED POEMS
1965–2000

Merrill Gilfillan

ADVENTURES IN POETRY

Cover sketch "Red Niobrara" by Merrill Gilfillan
Back cover photograph of Merrill Gilfillan
in Iowa City, Iowa, by John Deason © 1968
Book design by *typeslowly*
Printed in Michigan by McNaughton & Gunn

Adventures in Poetry titles are distributed to
the trade through Zephyr Press by Consortium
Book Sales and Distribution [www.cbsd.com] &
SPD [www.spdbooks.org]

9 8 7 6 5 4 3 2 FIRST PRINTING IN 2005

Adventures in Poetry
New York 🕷 Boston
www.adventuresinpoetry.com

Many poems in this collection appeared in the books *9:15* (Doones Press, Bowling Green, Ohio, 1970), *Truck* (Angel Hair, NYC, 1970), *Ten Cents* (Grunt Press, NYC, 1970), *Skyliner* (Blue Wind Press, Berkeley, 1974), *To Creature* (Blue Wind Press, 1975), *Light Years* (Blue Wind Press, 1977), *River Through Rivertown* (The Figures, Berkeley / Great Barrington, 1982), and *Satin Street* (Moyer Bell / Asphodel Press, Wakefield, RI, 1997). My long-running gratitude to Ray DiPalma, Anne Waldman, George Mattingly, Geoffrey Young, and the late Jennifer Moyer, proprietors of those presses. *River Through Rivertown* and *Satin Street* are included in their entireties. Several poems were published in the anthologies *None of the Above: New Poets of the USA*, edited by Michael Lally (The Crossing Press, 1976) and *The Angel Hair Anthology*, edited by Anne Waldman and Lewis Warsh (Granary Books, 2001). "Rita" was printed as a broadside by Blue Chair Press, as was "Finding the Islands" by Stele Editions, both from the DiPalma atelier.

Thanks to the editors of the following magazines where some of the works were printed: *Shelter; The North Stone Review; Strange Faeces; Doones; Just Before Sailing; The World; Suction; Clothesline; Chicago; The Harris Review; Sunshine; Nadine; Telephone; The Red Mavis Review; Buffalo Stamps; Streets and Roads; Blue Pig; This; Big Sky; Rocky Ledge; New Letters; The Grosseteste Review; New Blood; House Organ; InFolio; Five Finger Review; Hot Bird Mfg.;* and *o-blek.*

And affectionate thanks to Jack Collom and Christopher Mattison for valuable counsel regarding this project.

Table of Contents

Early Work {1965–1975}

Rita

My friend the violin
of my friend Poulenc a man
of the bees it's fine
to be back in America
after 800 years
of near Paradise
out front the Bijou
and everyplace else
even for ten minutes
toward the factory
the hard way
                    holding
your ears above your body
lips cherry red

An Ingratiation
(WCW)

Things out the window:
snow, a shadowbox of trees
and hybrid midwestern houses.
On second looking, a yard
of rotting clothesline someone tied
to the right-angle box elder limb,
and modest half-moons of snow
caught right-side-up in each
branch fork.
Just short of the garden site
a row of retired posts
where an old fence stood
leads the eye to the back-
porch of a modern woman
who shakes rugs among
the empty milk bottles.
Small things move by the window:
birds, all juncos, flirt
between weeds and snow;
the witch hazel flexes
its waxy fingers, the last
of the yellow things;
and there goes Williams,
metal-breathed into the suburbs
with his peaked straw hat
and his sore-thumbed shirt —
all the frail *non sequiturs*
at once.

Locusts, 1965

We skirted the river for two hours
before finding a bridge to Kentucky.
Once in, civil war monuments began
to sprout determined and lean
from beds of artificial flowers.
The splotchy cast-iron heroes strained
a last post-mortem convulsion
for the "border states"
in the tiny Appalachian towns, each
a surprise, thin-rooted mold busy
in the cracks of the mountains'
wishy-washy fate.
We drove at random for a week.
We said we could breathe there,
fall into any year at all.
                    North in Wheeling
we found the city fogged
with seventeen-year locusts, rampant
in their uncanny year of love:
resurrected red-eyed fossils
coating the trees, swamping our voices.
Layers of them covered the streets
so thick that only the older residents,
the veterans, would move.

Finding the Islands

Reconvening, stumbling out
of the wet trees with our houses on
when the ice was over,

how sure we were of no more
nights, fresh meat and melons,
parking lots to the inland

steady as grainfields.
Our lake was new water, views
of an ocean through clean whiskey.

Since Christmas, maps had held
the tables down; it was *that* difficult,
neighbor said, 10,000 miles,

no valentine can reach so far
and not be blown home ragged. Then
there was rain and no-name, morning

hurt the pock-marks of our beach
where we have just left those bushes
and stand up stretching,

the tents are down, legs out
from under the table, man walking,
men looking for wives.

Soneto (The Sky above Woolworth's)

From humdrum cirrus a radical swell
of mare's tail, middle right.   Pink tiles.
Yesterday miles of brown and dappled horses
with serious soldiers on top downtown.
A quick frisk at the National Palace.
Attica in the evening news.
The day before frigate birds swung out
over the coast above women washing clothes
and goats asleep or concentrating in the weeds.
2 men waved their hats in the distance, one
a fire-eater from the city, and his brother.
They were speaking Spanish to each other
and live near the cockatoos. All the latter-
lunar half of it bathed in easy golds and blues.

Mexico City, 1971

A Rune

A mathematics in your stance
resembles permanence

and lies. That was sleepy northbound Shakespeare
in your mouth.   Now on down

to find and cross Clinch, Roan
Mountain, up from here. That is South.

Proposed Elegy for Hart Crane

What a place for a garden,
pain like a pocketful of mints,
we live on each other.

As if an immigrant family crossed
some mysterious brightly colored bridge
and wandered into this lung-like valley
selling hot sandwiches and aerial photographs
of the Aztec dead we live on each other.

Nothing was planned without noise;
after dark the siren comes on in sheets,
she turns over loudly.
                              I think I could paint
when her back's turned.
                              Her back.

Or walk a little farther upstream
testing the furniture and the hair
in this area.
                    Yes it's a beautiful country,
flowerlike and huge, all the more graceful
when you consider it's rolling
and our many coffees rarely spill
but sometimes it takes itself away.

Rock River Serial

Some hot tea,
    tying the horses,
        who loves who?

Hair, an excuse
    for travel. Small hand
        an excuse for travel.

You belong there,
    stranger
        gathered at the knee.

Chas. Spand, The Paramount,
Richmond, Indiana, 1929

Alpacas have worn a groove in the floor
circling through tables peddling fruit or magazines
from their saddlebags. Avocados. Northern Spies.
Foreign Affairs. Don't bead me with your eyeball.

It reminds me of tomato juice. Which doesn't mix
with coconut melba. A faint sky blue shows in through
the window, right out of Audubon's *Mammals*: the mole
                              portraits,
at least two stellar scapes from a radical inspiration

so planted in another register and so blisteringly
childlike I threw up both my hands and yelled. Dime store
blues, mixed in a maple burl bowl obviously,
Siberian fashion. Blues of hungry sled dog eyes

mixed in a herring can and washed down with glacier water.
Moles up against it. Don't bead me with your eyeball.
The piano starts.
Alpacas quietly disappear through a door at the back.

To Syngman Rhee

I got restless picturing your ankles
the color of peach pits sunning on window sills,
too big to fit in small boy's ear.

Verdi

for Jayne

Hottest day of the year for Ukrainians,
they've forgotten to take their coats off for
the 23rd consecutive New World summer,

    nods to each other.
                 High up, white
in the blues, a few sea-birds are coasting
around over New York.
             Fact,
that on days like this one, or two, hot, clear —
asphalt shines like water to them: pockets of
Venice, dazzling white teeth, Italian garbage …

    Just the opposite —
    March 5th and my imagination's …
    Massachusetts plates, BL8-888 …

Not Verdi,
and to speak several words of American on the same day —
low-key, belly-country American near the Atlantic
Ocean,
        clear,   smoking,
           at you,   on television,
        maybe ten miles from here.

from 3 or 4 Mathematicians

She's got the flecks all over alright.
Some chain wires the thousand meals yelling
carp in her diary. Some station. Some anthropologist
is interested in those flecks as possible
signs for "some sleet" or "some hail."

A Vision

This time of day a year ago
I was turning south habitually
toward Ixtung along a highway bordered
with calypso cut from pure banyan,
close to what was once a river
reflecting the heart.

Chained to smoky poincianas
to hold off the lighter jungle, greyhounds
stretch in the dew and hawks come out
of the half light to register my roadster
from small caves perched high
in the strangler figs, and later

I pull into Jubal stiff and thirsty
for snapper under wine and garlic
served with off-white cheeses on a bluff
in the rhumba section, dancing close to the heart
arranged as more suburbs. Boilers, churches.

A serious person.
An old job at the Rose Cooperative.
The job, the only one I ever died
for — Roses and spending money!
So crystalline I shot from vice-exchequer
to front-line driver in less than a week and drew
the long-stem barrio route, where when they bought
you knew they'd be fed to the children cold,
approached like artichokes, but sweeter.

The rose truck.
That was politics in bloom
wheeling up to the high curbs in a drizzle,
firing a bandaged 12 gauge in the air.
Then we poured out for edible beauty like bats
and stormed the pink bars fed,
educated, beaten, raped, bankrupt, bombed and robbed
calm at the roots, the parquetry.

Steady pageantry work. At first
I never knew whether to wash before or after.

Riveters built low on the roof
with long-stems for lunch waiting in coffee cans
at the foot of the ladder, I remember them
against the sky. Madame du Calme waves from her bike.
I'll go away with her for her sidecar.

The older man who mined the Parthenon as a boy
scientist, about to drown in milk, he never bought any.
I admire him from a distance as he glides through
the dairy stalls. He has 50 dreams.

One of them I recognize from general afternoons
spent trying to find a place to whiz in Midtown broke
and stupid. Heh,
my little feesh calls buzzards down for the juices.

By the time I locate Rega it's morning again.
He sees me against the chintz so early
with muck all over my linens and sun at my back.

Parrots are out. We ride to the ocean
with knapsacks of heavy native beer on the donkey
to smoke in peace, and drink, and figure:

Library detective dead in the stacks.
Opera scatters from his delicate open hands.
From the stains we can see that he smoked
holding cigarettes between his middle fingers.
Probably genteel.

The other body is that of a woman I have seen
many times on the street. About 65, homeless, wearing
the same red toeless heels, old and loose enough
that one nail has grown out of each foot
to hold them on. A book strapped to one thigh.

To Elizabethans

They're planning a fair
or a festival, which is fine
if you're not a slave or a criminal,
and talk about the details
in a neighborhood replete with full canal
by which much later in the afternoon
holsteins spread out to see
an oceanliner. But I remember
absolutely nothing from my childhood
to make me think it's over.
Silk cravats wound around a tobacco plant,
nothing like that. No obsidian bicycle chains
buried under leaf piles either.
The guests-to-be shine
and toast sheer spiritual volume poised
in tenements and embassy buildings
blown from a single sandstone block,
and hand drums behind a happiness
notorious for blazing sunsets from the rim
of its pore, matched only by waiting
in line in a cut-rate place
under a live hotel on 47th Street buying gum
and 69 cent platinum nail clippers.
To which I dedicate the gum.

May

Gypsies
paused in a clearing
at the smell of new levis
and onion grass, drive on.

Idée Fixe et Bonne

Born, a noise
to professors of Navajo
at the Peking Institute
for Species Amalgamation.
China doesn't seem to care, but does
and in New York it's everywhere
by sundown. Mythical hairs
stand up on the neck of a tattooist
in back with the pastel jellies.
A gift to crowded parts
of the universe from cities.

Cadillac Mountain, Maine

for Fran Winston

I feel so good today I might even join the Cadillac
Mountain Sunrise Club. Every day they pack a breakfast
and climb the mountain in time for dawn, then you eat
and everyone trickles back to earth with a dazed foreign
look.

They're building a causeway or something down the
beach, a crane and dozens of faded blue denim specks
hurrying around.

Throbbing bass line. There aren't many mountains so
close to ocean in this country. You could probably get
work there if you want to.

I don't want to.

Platte River

Out here, a pretty remote stretch, it looks like most of the rivers between, or rather in a square made by Nebraska, the Rio Grande (and maybe farther south), Arkansas and the foothills of the Rockies. I'll give up my idea of collecting sample vials from famous rivers of the Plains because they all evoke the same picture: broad brown lazy tintype under the sun, one dog in a slow straight line to the west.

The real, chemical combination is sex and geography (kicks her sand-colored bikini underpants into the dunes); what freaked Whitman deep down. It's a loving landscape and the small red pennants fly. If he had had more concrete lovers, maybe one in every place he hung around.... If Hart Crane had been born 50 years earlier America would have its own Verlaine-Rimbaud thing and one of the most incredible psycho-sexual geographies in the world.

Tanager

There's no sun today
                    Sunday May 10
my father's birthday
                    but we don't need any more
anymore
                    This afternoon   he's 60

In my upstairs highschool bedroom
                              I'm watching
a green striped dress
                    float a blond girl
down some steps
                    across the street
He's reading
                    on my broken highschool bed

        The Sonnets

                    *

If I were William Carlos Williams
        I'd say
                "ahh" and "ah ha"

Ahh and Ah ha
                    anyway

The Starfish at Heart

When the partridge eats
the partridge berry ...

I.

A MANTLEPIECE

The shadow of a light plane, zip,
a woman strolling in her side yard admiring
the zinnias and drying her nails, hands
held lightly up as if about to touch piano
keys, and I, we saw it.

2.

THE WORK (THE JUNE)

Catalpa blossoms dropping
all over town. A broom crew
shovels them up.

3.

THE OHIO AT LOUISVILLE

A hundred forty Boones
in the phonebook. One Keats.

4.

THE POT LIP

They liked
to hear the neighbor
rap her spoon against
the pot lip.

5.

THE MINIATURE

"Were I in that audience
I'd be applauding still."

from **Horseshoe**

And insects too of the prairies
                              my love (too)
                    in an embarrassing way:

            Icy ticking of big racing Schwinns:

                    You sound like that,

        This a turbulence (my love) too …

Preface to **Earth**

Certain experiences enter our lives by nostalgia only, and stay there, sometimes growing with a slow cautious warmth into mainstays.

Native islanders call this kind of experience "Fish Crow," after the elusive bird of that name.

I write letters on this subject to London, New York, Paris, and quite a few smaller places in Ohio, Michigan, Colorado (Colorado), and Iowa, where my friends have been.

I've only seen 3 fish crows in my entire life, all in early dawn of April, 1964, roosted on a shiny barkless elm standing in a light drizzle just outside those creamy cities.

A Romany

Aircraft finished highseas piracy.
This from desert folk when their sandpaintings
blow. Sharon Renee Carter, deep Romany,
blew.

A Head at the Window

The huge head of a huge woman. The size of her face alone amazes me: it's at least two feet thick in any direction, radiating the poise of cognac in capitalist magazines. I live with this woman and amigos swing from the bridges, in the name of What — Aroma? Japanese swordsmen throw their brains a thousand miles in any direction twice a day to do knuckle exercises beneath it. The Greeks spit and gave it emphasis.

Against the Crow Indians

You with the only pompadours on North America
    and a taste for jewelry
You spent all your money on dentalium shells
    and ate dogs.
You hated the popular Sioux.
The French knew, they called you Beaux Hommes.
Which translates "Army Scouts."
You could have slippt off into some undiscovered
    corner of Montana and kept your horses alive,
    beading the soles of your shoes, combing body-
    length hair all over some corner of Montana
    where I could live out my youth in simple
    honest luxury.

Août 72

Limousine,

I thought I was unloved,
alone at last, then a friend
of my mother arrives
in the brain fields

and continues to my body
by immaculate zebra skirting
coy plastic surf. Agh. Mystery.
Low porcelain hills open

to frenzy but generally cool
we passed a shepherd crapping
in the woods, holding
his hand-carved flute

in his teeth on the way
to a small party in the foothills,
cars parked along the dusty road
among them the cherry Packard,

above them rocky mountains
and from here you can see dull red
and green blurs here and there
where grenades rolled out

from under the camouflage way
way up. O O birds before your minds
took over. O O eager looks
through cold clear water

and priceless navy bodies creased
and figured from sleeping
on the rope. Roy took a ride
on a chrome hay wagon.

The larger of the two
was an aspiring building, vacant
and inspiring above the poonta
poonta poonta of the gypsum works

we saw where we stopped
to sell the rubies. Inside
was a tight yellow room
with well-worn flimsy white trim

and muffled gold curtains
shattered about knee-level, a row
of circular windows facing directly
onto the bay. I pour a whiskey

and stand in the far one
inhaling salt air and half listening
to the high thin whine of shellfish
feeding close around the reef

at sundown. A tuba-faced man
gets out of a dark convertible
and limps toward the door
in a slight hurry,

pink dacron shirt steaming
under a blue Muslim smoking jacket
like an orchid. Mr Bertoni — Mr Khan.
TV light looks weird

through igloo walls
and the cord disappearing off
across the ice looks even stranger,
X bent over the hotplate

melting down the rubies,
dictating lurid memos for the Hong Kong
plan: return to popular western harbors
underwater to salvage tons

of opium syrups ditched
by moonlight coating the floor
of the outer bay to be traded in capitals
as acne creme for sweet industrial glues.

And meantime off Gibraltar
hundreds of swollen cellos just waiting
for a man of vision and friends
to finance the new music.

Then that entirely different time
in the North outside a tavern
with spaceheaters wired into the dash
of the pickup parked next door.

Ah. Ooo. Ah.
Mango trees unwinding, Z bent
over the barbecue melting down
the blubber. The lava is hot.

Señor reappears from the basement
with a crusty ammunition box
of vintage goatskin shoes
as he puts it, on the sexual horizon.

If I gather my senses and both hands
I can see its streetlamps on but broken,
neighborhoods reeking of zen, money, rabbits
and Señor. Guano barge ahoy!

Although we share a minimal
commonground I absorb his polka tastes
in strategy and music while he picks up
my preference in views,

cheap shrimp and weather, long
before and after dinner walks diamond-shaped
from cards or baseball, east, and up
and over feathered Inca racing dogs to who.

River Through Rivertown

{1982}

MARCH (BABUSHKA)

The kind of day submarine crews
dream of.

One Morning

April,
bad to be better armed
than the gods. Good
not to be entirely empty-handed.

So
how are they
going to lift those granite blocks,
with a crane?

Morning green,
old copper in Spring.

There's even
a voodoo stamp behind one shoulder,
a Sun. In a matter of minutes, bells
will ring, to the temperature.

May it ride
between minus 50 and fire.

2.

A whiff, a dose
breathy about the matrix,
You are partly sun,
partly citizens Nobody knows.

Born of sphagnum picker
by shady alchemist out of raving beauty
and dazed Charlestonaire.

Standing there.   Hungry?

I know a place for rooftop squab,
cheap,
packed in snow
driven deep into the Atlantic
by its fluid past.

A noisy little place
a few feet from the Titanic memorial.
You are absolutely clear.
You wash and run these streets.

3.

FLORA

April, foods from trucks
and bikes

suspiciously resembling rickshaws
(taboo).
They are stringing it out,
stretching it.
They are starting from scratch
in the flora. They are hauling in the herbs
and the spices. A packet of bee balm
beside bales of tarragon. Turmeric
and the bays. Heavily guarded saffron.
(I needed a hat. In an hour
on Orchard Street I found a small felt job
hanging from a nail in a dusty bin.
They said it was a headpiece
of the saffron gatherers, a light beret
with a thirty inch cord attached.
At the loose end a pouch, tiny lamé,
air-tight and claspable,
that originally served as receptacle
for the stigma tips
as they were trimmed from the flowers
and could be slipped conveniently
down the back, under the shirt
in heavy traffic or taverns.
This one was embroidered, pregunpowder gold
on brown. Renee swears
she saw one passing through downtown Herat
with a propeller on the crown.)
Red peppers spread on the flat beds
in open trays, red red.
They ride the collapsible statue:
To garlic,
bareback, high in the FM range.

4.

ONE MORNING

A long swim in unbroken water.

Are anchovies naturally salty, or is it all
in the brine? Al?

Dressed and combed I mingle with sleepy
ornithologists at the edge of the airfield. Calm,
sipping coffee from a gallon thermos, they were
waiting for a flight of jungle eggs, from the
interior.

5.

FOR FOLEY

Alchemy
reduced itself to chemistry
and counterfeiting.

The courtyard is in full voice.
A soprano running the scale. The bass
upstairs, recorders, harmonica
and slide guitar. A collapsible garden.

A table for two
near the front for the Equinox.

This is propaganda, a hill
in one eye. Circus horses graze
to one side: We might have been tuned
otherwise, to live by ear
in constant tone. Maybe a jammed diesel horn
anchoring all orbits. No no

no no no, she trills.

There would be wine at the curbs,
exploding cigars for the Winter Solstice,
the quietest day on the charts.

6.

What special delicacy
is served here, I wonder

                 Sora, Basho's friend

7.

Pidgin English
is pidgin English
for *Business English*.

It knows the old shopkeeper
adding columns with silvery 14 inch
nostril hair braided into a watercolor brush.
We swim in the same lagoon.
His canary yellow 7 running into the sum
is laced with semiaccidental Rorschach blue,
very lush.

Señor,
your ink blots remind me of a bus station floor.

Wayfaring strangers
knocking like radiators,
I still wonder where you've been
but I watch you less and less. Acquaintances:
solid atomic friends. No keys.
I hear in India you would be bathed now and then
by affectionate force. You know better.
I know where you sleep.

Men and women, different corner.
Checkout girls and garbagemen, passersby
caught by the slow moaning and groaning
from a one-up window on Broadway.
All of us stopped, ears cocked, eyebrows lifted,
even on tiptoe at the edge of dance.

Ha. On down the street.

Surface tension not today,
everyone's been around.
Dogs fight, the wind shifts —
flying fish — You're in a harbor town.

8.

SEAS

Mare Crisium..........................Sea of Crises
Mare Nectaris.........................Sea of Nectar
Mare Tranquillitatis..................Sea of Tranquility
Mare Serenitatis......................Sea of Planned Obsolescence
Mare Frigoris.............................Sea of Frigoris
Mare Imbrium............................Sea of Lip
Mare Vaporum............................Sea of Smoky Faces
Mare Nubium.............................Sea of See
Mare Foencunditatis....................Sea of Hot Loins
Mare Humorum...........................Sea of Grin
Seas.

9.

While we're on the centrifuge
imagine Glissando a mountain girl
beside it in the yard with Saturn
and Torelli on the screen
and several thousand grainy in between
too dim to see.

Or
T. at ease in the shade of an edible weed.
A corner on the kohlrabi deal.
To discourage rabbits during crucial weeks
he trains pigeons to fly soft and low,

to resemble hunting owls,
and sends them out over the fields.

A dangerous waiter at the Hoy.

Notre Dame,
DNA houndstooth mating like prairie chickens
(like mink!) lip-reading *Adieu*.

Source of storm and bar joke passing over.
(What did the moron tell the Mormon?)

Mild wonders of the far side without you.

10.

ANOTHER MORNING

By midmorning, seconds after we arrived and decided
to eat, the first fruit wagons were back. The vendors,
who had been waiting around the loading platform for
an hour Stan told us, filled their trays and started out to
work. There must have been 50 of them, all dressed the
same down to the finest blue and white detail, maybe
even brothers. It reminded me of the Buddha multiplying
himself to receive identical gifts from various gods with-
out offending any of them. They poured down the slope
to where we were resting. It was a small triumph for
perfectionism. Together, we felt like a full orangutang.
Smiling and scratching beside the tracks. When I think of
people I've known already my fillings ring.

11.

INSECTA

I read up on you in Fabre.

12.

Gaucho orbits.
Tick. Tick. Tick.
Translucent coils in perpetual mix.

Coincidentally
I move around the room in May
where I was born, there
for Hiroshima. It rocked the cradle,
Prince,
and temporarily revived
the ancient pleasures
of crossing and uncrossing the legs
at high speeds. Club car,
potato convoy, weather balloon.

Whose auspices are tidal,

Rich in the Vitamin Earthburn.
But I'd rather spend my money in the street.
Hot squab on a bed of catalpa leaves.

Whose auspices are tidal.

We will be visited in the night
by shirts so bright they draw us honeybees
and like it.

13.

ANOTHER MORNING

All the children I passed for 30 blocks
were the same age. A generation at 3, cities
seen from Berkeley, or Hoboken.

14.

FAUNA

Women in a half-circle
in kerchieves and shawls.
Facing the river in a half-circle
holding out the popcorn.
Low Belorussian pigeon calls.

An old friend stops by
with animals, and friendly eyes
reminiscent, lightly,
of that slight bulge they used to add
to public columns intimating
gracious strain.

He thinks
if they shifted the bulge to the top
the whole building would seem to float
a fraction off the ground.

How about the day
they will remember to find, say,
protosilk dust in Neanderthal ballrooms
under, say, the Parthenon?
They could probably use your idea.

We laugh, he disagrees.

15.

The eggs are cold, light yellow.

*

It sleeps all morning.

*

It comes on with the streetlights,
a couth.

New York
24 April 75, a.m.

Homage to Balzac

I.

I was contemplating the worm in the myth
that chose the century for its measure —
close behind fan dancers, overhearing a story.
John saw Paul come in, jumped up
and hurried across the dining room.
He caught up with him at the small bar nestled
in one end of the place, pulled out a kid glove
and slapped him across the face. Paul looked
for a minute then reached into his raincoat
for a glove of his own, slowly put it on
and caught John on the chin so hard
he demolished two heaping tables of pasta.
Talk about your mass at the foot of the diamond,
alligator pump in the midst of the stars.

2. WRITTEN IN "FERRAGUS"

And
What came directly from the stars
except North
and written Persian?
The latter constellations at noon,
rain so fine
it doesn't even dent the tea —

That's Persian, son: northern lights
to deepen wine: Men
with flaming heads. Kids climb trees
along the street to see.

3.

A birdcall artist plays
on the corner. He can do a woodthrush
that makes the shadows fall for 50 cents.
Time is the solo of space.

4. WRITTEN IN "LEVITICUS"

Will it blow
Or is it stuck in the lungs?

   (Send Harry —
      he has read Balzac.

Young sweet corn grows
under some of them.
Talk about your islands:
Talk about your lives in the night.
Your lost rubber glove
whose recent owner, under another one,
sighs *It was almost like part of my hand.*
Your speech to the lockpickers,
your feasts of all sizes,
solar instructions cooling on flagstone
(a kind of light according to the master).
Men should be like wolves, what wolves.
Hail Balzac:
Flies in the smoke rings. Dew on the chain.

The Rights of Man

1.

FLICKER FEATHERS

for a Fall wedding

Woman on the lawn with wine,
pick up summer for a broken book,
rinse your voice in aster
and the lace of Queen Anne,
stall for speechlessness,
kneel in the weeds, soak.

Man in the woods (a whiskey),
stamp, make noise over breakage,
take these five feathers, cornyellow
and horsehair brown, arranged
in a fan shape, finely pointed
and turning in your fingers, home.

2.

ST. VITUS

Eggs for breakfast, chicken
for dinner: the proverbial bending over
backwards to a weakness for the prehistoric —
then walking to the park like that,
where late sleepers are cutting their way
out of the bushes into sun or star

light. I'll gladly pay money for this
when I have to, but so far I got in free.
This morning it's daylight and my friends
are shaking. An old one shows me moss
lining a crease in his elbow.
I tell him about my Mexican tick bite
reappearing after two months
as a perfect figure eight on my instep.
It had been locked in the ice.
Later that same day I noticed fronds
sprouting from its intersection
and by midnight one very small aqua flower
bloomed. A hush fell but the whole thing
was gone in the morning.

3.

MANDALACRITY

for Jean Seberg

Beech woods silver from the bus:
Wash the window: Oak leaves
tattered by gunfire in the documentaries
no longer any good against the sun.
The voice of the thief laced
with the voice of the john.

                              Y'all.

That low-gear growl about
A Gorgeous Moray on a Pier:
'In Campeche they trade women

for those things.' Each,
single and undivided, does it all.

4.

ST. VICINITY

The hollow back
of the second rim of
the ridge. Dependable bluffs
at the junction. Pine-

clad coulee.
The bottom. A broad trail
running the valley crossing
and recrossing the stream.

Flats cut by runnels
broken by breaks.
The crest. The seep.
The dufus near the peak.

A swale. The pass.
The dip. A sandy spit
edged under shale cliffs.
A knoll overlooking

the meadow. Headwaters
fanning out in the foothills.
A right-sized canyon. The rise.
The lick in the glade.

5.

ANOTHER VERSION OF THE SAME

D. H. Lawrence is in pain.
His velveteen jacket is bright green.
His thoughts run to women.
Good man. Big heart. Big brain.

6.

MONT JOLI

for Gus

A red dawn woke everyone
on the right side of the train:
the first sharp flash above Gaspé
I think. I asked a porter
where we were: *Mont Joli:* three
of the sheerest: the little 't'
a digit in the river calling
children in from play: hair
yellower than porchlight: things
to Montreal: and back.
They rose in whispers up and down.
Mont Joli. Mont Joli, Mont Joli.

We'll make: Hoppin' John.

7.

THE BATTERY (EPITHALAMIUM)

for Betty and Roy

Ellis Island looks closer
than last time: You can see the Vivaldi & Co.
behind Virginia reels
if you shut your eyes. The harbor is fast and hungry
after a night of wind airing the palladium.
Barge to barge.
Today I'm witnessing a secret marriage:
I'm the Widow Edlin in *Jude the Obscure,* down off
the buggy (crusty miles) and into the chapel
to sit and hum, chat, laugh, look serious,
touch up my boots with a snap of the bandana.
A little of each: Eros
in general: the Well-placed Hand.

8.

THE RIGHT TO DANCE

You may mother may I
                        in Wm. Bartram
the possibility of meeting strangers
                        deep in the forest
giving away fawnskins
                        of wild honey.

                ★

(Big brown eyes:

                              Sleepy
little space station town.

            9.

PROPINQUITY

Place the imperfections
at the feet of the queen,
                    leave town
the back way in case they implode.
Fried potato clouds and then a single dogwood
for the road. Wild birds call ·
from a gully: R
SVP.
        Prince Valiant is good this week:
his son is about to spring him
from slavers.
                    Watch the farmers. Ummm,
a hot pie cooling in a window. Hungry
an hour later.
                    Wave as you pass.
(Propinquity.
I saw a house-with-camellias named that
down south, checked it later
in the dictionary.)
                    A day-o not
to go see the two-headed calf.

10.

ST. VICINITY 2

The ford, the face,
the eddy. The gap
at the bend. Arroyos
by day. Timbered

point not far above
the mouth. The sap.
A long swell. The run.
The drop. A fork.

Rills at the source.
An oak-opening. The hog-
back again. The mesa,
set. The bayhead.

A grassy bench
on the lower slope of
the butte. A dry wash.
The dork. A cove

on the lee. The spring.
The wallow. The falls.
The range from a ville
in the gulch. The roll.

11.

TANTRICITY

for Channette

Whose green of the Osage Orange:
'You don't just walk around down here
calling everyone *amigo.'*   Up the run
the last angel fell to feather hunters.
A marble X marks the spot.
Like Chopin's grave it's Swept by Women.

We make: Hoppin' John.

12.

SAN LUIS OBISPO

Three dance
            to a car radio
in the parking lot —
                        twisted cedar
of the bunch buys food.
                        (From over here it sounds
a little like the *Robin's Egg Blues.)*
                              Then
they drive to New Yo.
                        They're happy
because they have a long way to go.

Corvée

I.

A tree of heaven nods
in the breeze. A dog barks
across town. A squat brick building
sits dimly lighted.

Rows of silver tanks glow
beyond the tracks below
a water tower. Nighthawks over
people in line. A bat

through the arc light.
A rooster crows to the east.
A click. Then the robins,
and the train.

Snap your fingers,
The day opens on
backyards pretty much as
you left them: the river

still in its bed and the late moon
wearing blue still up there:
the pair of bronze goat boys
in the parlor pretty much as

you left them, staring
at their funny feet: territories
re-opened like melons
in a field, re-settled,

re-minded from afar: *Hai yah:*
Marching orders: Fungo army.
The Elvis look-alike still
sound asleep under a tree.

2.

FROM "AURELIA"

by Gérard de Nerval

I went to the Tuileries, the gates were locked. I
walked along the quais and strolled through the Lux-
embourg Gardens. Then I circled back for dinner with a
friend. Later I went to St. Eustache, where I knelt before
the Virgin and thought of my mother. My tears relieved
me and on the way out I bought a silver ring. Then I
went to see my father; he wasn't in, so I left a bouquet
of daisies by the door. I walked to the Jardin des Plantes.
It was crowded. I stopped for a while to watch the hippo
splash around, then went into the Museum of Natural
History. All the reconstructed monsters reminded me of
The Flood; as I left a downpour hit the gardens.

3.

Split open the French bread,
spread it with cream cheese
and Sopchoppy honey, eat it
to one of the Bachs in the next room
filling the Venetian blinds
like a sail —

                  dented silver platter
by Sherpa —

                  to the Art of the Fugue,
its Portuguese and Mexican cowboys
who migrated to Hawaii
for the late 19th Century cattle boom
and brought Pacific steel guitar
back here around the bend of the 20th
where it hulaed with the blues
and flourished till World War II,
especially, they tell me,
in Chinese restaurants.

4.

Lining up.
Chopping suey. Turning
into trees. Falling down.
Throw together a Greek salad:
villages pop up all around.

5.

Lining up to wait and see you,
palomino moon.
                    Lining up
to see this technicolor postcard,
a simple thing, at your service:
Louyse Moillon's *Still Life with Cherries.*
And gooseberries. With strawberries
in the background, and a dewy sprig
of currants tossed in at the
last minute.
                    To make it a city
instead of a town.

Red-Haired Boy

I.

SOUTH AND DEPEYSTER

Copy shop girls are singing a work song.
I don't know the man on my left.
His jacket is warm, his eyes are bright
given a winter sky. Ones to my right
or behind either.
Coffee shop girls are singing a bean song.

2.

AS I WRITE IT'S A JUNE AFTERNOON

Saturday: Nights I walk around this village of a thousand
houses above a small river. Most people are in bed. The
summer trees are full and heavy, dark within, submarine;
on some side streets they hang so low I have to stoop.
Now and then a muffler breaks the silence. If he makes all
three traffic lights he can pass through in a minute and a
half.

Of the thousand a majority are frame buildings painted
white. Some are brick, here and there a stone or stucco
with its lights out. They stand within classic cross-shaped
arteries: High and Main, extending in cardinal directions.

After how many walks like this, finally, they sit there where they belong: It is a real *village*, as in longhouse, wickiup, yurt. The water arrives at the sinks for a small fee. Loose clapboards are tacked down. Of the thousand, I was born, more or less, in one; lived in three; have been inside maybe a hundred; stood on the porches of several more.

Sunday: Tonight Mars and Saturn pass exceptionally close together. It made the papers. They hang bright just west of overhead ¾ of an inch apart to the human eye. But the yards around town are empty of people — mosquitoes are bad this year. And every dull endless repetition, every cycle, clockwork and cliché are invaluable as oxygen tonight. Each old woman moving some unused object from one part of her room to another; each half glass of tepid water before bed; the chiseled names in the graveyard. Apt, Fate, Askew. Wood, Bush, Buck, Munk. Earlywine, Overturf, Underwood. Ireland, England, Poland. Jaycox, Laycox, Brown and Green. The night is *full*. The town is *full*. It was full in 1945. The war is over. The troops are coming home. To one man that meant her husband is coming home. He's in Cleveland right now waiting for a train south. Shoot her in a busy restaurant on Main Street, walk a block north to the Globe Hotel and shoot yourself. This is a sad example.

Monday: With a name like Earlywine you could ... what? Become a chief or headman of sorts? Ideally you could turn out the first, freshest vintage in town and walk the streets. Crocus, or lilac, wine. That sort of Synch went

out with animal speech. Although somewhere there
must be a baker named Baker who can lead you to a
talking mule.

The circulation is holding clear. The cycle still obvious
tonight from water tower to faucet to drain. The lights
go off. The pipes are full. The whole sewer system glows
in the dark.

Mother always says, 'Put some butter on it.'

3.

THE WABASH AT NEW HARMONY

She bicycled by.
As matron saint of back doors
she'll be kind. One slamming down the block's
her show of force.
                    River through Rivertown —
A name for a horse.

4.

UP THE MILK

Find it on a map,
chart it by the cottonwoods,
the dark line down the valley
worth an ocean, the lode.
Milk River immersion cures neuritis,

neuralgia, the shakes, the shits and the law.
The bad dream. Trims fat,
cools greed. Grows hair years later.

*

    I was killing a hot afternoon in a Browing bar, wait-
ing for the bus, when a mean-looking man who knew
everyone came in with a camera.
    'See this camera? I got it for 10 bucks.'
    'Hey, you got any film in that thing?'
    'Sure I got film in it.'
    'Why don't you take a picture of us?'
    'Lemme see it a minute.'
    'I paid 10 dollars for it, from Frank.'
    'There isn't any film in this thing.'
    'How about a picture of Jim and me?'
    'There isn't any film in it, look.'
    'Let's get everybody in it. Let's all go out front,
whadyasay.'
    The five of us — two blue-eyed curly-haired brothers,
a wrinkled handsome old man with pigtails, the cook
(sober, whispering the whole time, 'The damned thing's
empty') and I — filed outside like schoolboys, around
the corner of the building and posed against main street,
old style, serious with the chins up.
    Click.

*

Curve of the earth.
    Bring bucket.

66

5.

DOWN THE SUWANNEE

A soft hook.
A perfect gentleman. So-and-so
settled in a hamlet off the turnpike
making a modest living
translating for the highway patrol
when they pull in
the occasional non-English-speaking speeder.
A vaguely familiar face streaming tears.
The world's foremost memory musician,
master ecstatician, done in at breakfast
by the surprise appearance of his long-lost
baby spoon beside his grapefruit. Girls women
by now; natural features rechristened
where necessary. A still life
starring a bowl of dried duck dung
(ancient source of purple dye)
and some of those daisies.

6.

KITESTRING TO QUIPU

Great Bend: First view of the Arkansas, a flimsy one
through binoculars from route 56 above town: just the
sudden off-green of the bottom a mile or so below. The
great bend itself, the river reconsidering to the southeast

toward Wichita. Radio was playing the *Florida Suite*.

Wichita, I understand, is the home of Einstein's brain, what's left of it, housed there by a dedicated patholo- gist named Thomas Harvey who is reportedly running tests to determine its uniqueness, if there is one. The cerebellum, the cerebral cortex and other fragments are preserved in mason jars in a cardboard box — all the pieces remaining after the original dissection in 1955 that pronounced the organ's size, weight and structure normal. (All this with Einstein's blessing in advance, of course.) But Harvey wasn't satisfied. The Einstein family expects an official report in due time but so far the doctor is secretive, apparently working his way through the bil- lion brain cells one at a time after hours.

Larned: Three weak but steady channels meander among sandbars and young cottonwoods.

Levels of hearsay: Glancing out the window this morning I see, in well-grazed run-of-the-mill pasture land, a six-by-six foot patch of high grass and weeds hap- hazardly fenced off long ago with barbed wire — nothing visible within, probably a bad spring or abandoned well. I think instantly of the evening star, a light ritual with fish fry, woodsmoke, watercolors and simple open laughter.

East of Kinsley: Twelve feet wide, deep-looking.

The river isn't short of fans. A passer-by was having lunch below the bridge, a man driving to Oklahoma City with a remarkable voice pitched like a six-year-old's. Coming from a 40-year-old body in a maize summer suit it made a catchy toy train whistle music. He enjoyed the

Einstein story. In 1934 his uncle had been manhandled and tied in a small Iowa town where he was mistaken for John Dillinger.

Dodge City: Completely dry! I drove twice across what had to be the bridge — spanning a wide gravel bed bordered by federal flood-control walls — and even went a little farther out of town thinking there must be some mistake. In a quonset roadhouse where two dozen young men watched a local girl run the pool table (she could have led us howling across the plains by night) a man said the water was diverted for irrigation, had been for six or eight years. "It's still running, but you can't see it."

Cimarron: Nothing. A broad dry bed showing a few cattails.

Ingalls: Nada. Bed overgrown with sunflowers.

Garden City: Zilch. Cottonwoods dead, their bark falling off.

Lakin: Dry as a bone.

Syracuse: Greener from afar ... and running. Eight feet wide, very shallow. It calls for the lawn chair: *Sough, sough:* Small flags to be designed and planted: the Truckee at Reno, the condom factories at Charlotte: Musical notes on seersucker staff. A baggy suit of this material for the Harpo Marx in Albert.

Holly: Two healthy channels.
    If the brain proves regular ... it must have been the hair.

7.

CAPE MAY

In a beach scene
words breaking on world.
We asked for a glass of water
as the convent and got it.
Late May. Striped tents
not-there-last-night-there-today
aglow in the pines. Toothpick cutters.
They come in jeeps with Finnish knives
and small cardboard boxes.

8.

HORSE HEAVEN HILLS

They deserve a cheese to remember.
One that lasts on the fingers,
wrapped in local yellow grasses
for the view. One that wakes you
gently in the night
and might well get you arrested
in a tender part of town. Concentrate,
you only saw them by moonlight.
A Buddha-Who, a keeper, at home
on the bread. And well-named.
I can't remember the time or the place
but the cheese, was *Heat-seeker*.

9.

PORT-AUX-BASQUES

A Newfoundland barked on the dock.

10.

CORPUS CHRISTI

In old decks
there's a young queen
climbing a stepladder to her horse
and half the corner kids know
how to take the birthmark on her knee:
A blessing of the fleet:
Sweet blarney-by-the-sea. Let
every nook and inner ear and sail open
to its air tonight.
Very South and Depeyster.
Cans shine to be kicked.
Supper to be sung for.
The heart to be held up to the light.

II.

RED OAK DESK

Monday: I heard Henry Miller lived in Santa Monica — information that later proved false — and that he frequented the park mornings despite failing strength necessitating a walker. It's a busy park, long and narrow and subdued by the faint chatter of mockingbirds in shrubbery and droning planes as vague as the mountains in the distance. Many convalescents take the sun there, playing shuffleboard or gazing out to sea. I watched a bus slowly, surely tear off a WALK/DON'T WALK sign as it squeezed around a tight corner. No Henry, but as might be expected more than one man resembling his younger self from afar — his kind of hat, glasses....

Tuesday: Arabic graffiti, predominant in the park, is a pleasant change for the eye, as are the remnant frame bungalows around LA, providing curious soft spots among the stucco. Their dry "Little Rascals" yards. The slight adrenalin rush at every glint of a distant wheelchair nearly made me give up my search. But it is honorable, a magpie told me, and after an hour strolling the length of the park I discreetly swept the crowded porch of a retirement hotel across Ocean Boulevard with my binoculars.

Wednesday: Each morning there was a Japanese painter working cross-legged under the same palm tree, painting rapidly with a palette knife. Not more than a minute or two per sheet, and a sizable stack of finished work beside him. Each day a cold-water vigor and a distant smile, con-

sistently painting the same view, facing north up the
coast. During the two-day fire in the mountains last
week he no doubt painted the smoke.

12.

WEST FELICIANA

One of the names
not to be changed.

13.

SCRANTON

You'd like to see an Appaloosa for instance.
Twice a year one passes through
in an open trailer. Dark, almost blackberry
across the haunches.
                              Guinea stinkers?
Scranton,
like a glove. There are 3,000 varieties
of leaf tea. Richard II dined with 10,000 daily.
The boxcar serials total 2,329,405 —
Parodis and De Nobilis finite high and dry
onshore.

          Try one of mine.

Satin Street
{1997}

Crayola Da Gamba

Aspen leaves
the size of dimes —
as dimes: whippets
without the
within: Days heavy
on the trumpet
voluntary: Days
pitch black and maize.
I had a smooth yoyo
those colors once.
We're talking about the sun.

Mustard mare,
four girls in yellow on her —
They're talking about the sun.

The Illinois Above Grafton: Fu

Tiers of hills, chartreuse-the-drink to forest green: whistle up the berry with animal cracker seeds: Set in ring, for chinaman, the one in the magazine squinting into the camera either laughing or crying, and later in two or three dreams. In the latter there was always a grain of delicious-looking rice stuck to one of his mustache hairs: an idea almost: heron in tree.

And a river, the Illinois, curving slowly out of sight to the south.

Solstice Letter

for Ray and Elizabeth DiPalma

I think of you
as the tarts come out
of the oven — Ohio butternuts
from Ohio butternut
trees — and last summer's
ash seeds rattle
in the wind beyond
the window: small
bat-of-the-eye pleasures
of winter. Deep. Distilled.
Discardable. Like frying potatoes
near the solstice (a big batch,
the Main Course, silverdollars
with onion flashed
to chestnut); Scotch,
no rocks; and travelessness,
the art of going nowhere
for a month or two.
                              Last May
we drove to Arizona, sent
a paper plane down Canyon
de Chelly and spent days
steeping in the Chiricahuas,
the border country
crawling with humming
and other birds. Those cool
unsuspected canyons

tucked high above
the desert, the stillness,
their poise will take your breath
away. Dawn and dusk
cool air flows up or down them
like a tide; the sycamores
sigh. And on through the umber
to El Paso and Juarez
for blankets — those shrimp
and calamari vendors with their tubs
of ice deserve
a hungry painter — and north
through the panhandle
and east across Kansas
(foaming with early peonies
and late lilacs), skirting
the Ozarks and dropping
into Kentucky for Burgoo,
to Ohio, where we were given
butternuts
Many hours in the Cracking,
and back,
full of space and scattered barbecue
and ready for more
and more of the continent
slowly taking solid form
within.

But now in December
we have the travelessness,
the distillation, the stirring

and the basting, leaving
one's wandering figment to carry on,
miniature Tarzan/
Astaire hybrid always out there
in the nonvoluntary imagination,
On Duty, crossing
and recrossing, fresh towns
at daybreak, with no baggage:
just a golfball-size nugget
of good parmesan
to be grated over anything
and everything at all.

Nights I whistle him in
like a dawg.

And sundown today
(I'll think of you
when those hens come out
of the oven), sundown
this year, you have *word*,
finally, and we have
a sky
the color of milk
that blueberries
have been in; mountains
to the immediate west,
their pines in intricate silhouette
this time of day; and coffees,
hot coffees: the gentle Kona,
a rare New Guinea "A."

Water and Song 1981

for MR

An early sky still up
for grabs: flock settles
on the chance-medley phrase
                    three from Plaquemines —
the lark beat, the plumber
in it.
            Plumbers see
what doctors used to: the cheese with one bite
missing on strange tables and the dead mouse
under the stairs: take their pay in water
then disappear.
                        Kachina repairmen
dress like chimney sweeps: backseats full of
feathers and weeds: take their pay in talk
about the weather and dance on.
                        This springlike

Fall a shift of hemispheres:
Great-trade-routes-in-the-wings
in the wind: Pearls for oysters: oils
for an autumn scene
where a million winesaps roll
to bins —
                (From rare earth
mostly —
            (*three from Plaquemines*

Rain Along the Kaw

Racks of punts or rapier sculls
at ease just yards from river:
damp decorum no tongues hang out from.
Scows.
Days like this remind me of the forties:
Seven elms: a *week* of trees the light rain
handles like a veil. Faintly muddy flow
faint news from upstream west
(as opposed to empty northwind).
Have you heard —
When a boar is gored in heaven
a good man drops on earth?
The godwits have arrived, Keewatin
and God's Mercy Bay?
As prospects for survival as a peasant fall
prospects for survival as a bandit rise?

Winterberry

for MCG

Mornings we think up
the Spotted Horse road:
January morning force majeur:
The Spotted Horse road a thousand miles
west in imaginary April, or July: sagehens
strutting slowly through the sage —
chay, chay —

think of it
isometrically, just so over breakfast,
two people thinking same place
the way others clink glasses: the hills,
the hens thinking water, highstepping down
from the sage hills, elbow
to elbow at the pool.

We think of it, hold it
just above our familial heads
while we look at the winterberry:
crooked sprigs stuck in a cutglass cruet,
hard red berries winterburned
and wrinkled on a muck-black twig,
charcoal and scarlet on a cold week
sere as desert.

(Middle of the night I awoke
thinking two things at once: grand aerial view
of nocturnal beech forests
still bearing flaxen winter leaves,
their noble continuum across
the eastern continent, beatific presence
interlaced as lace — and Toni
unheard of twenty years
slinking into an unspecified steakhouse
in a tight black dress.) The two things
at once.

Bipeds: We look
at the winterberry, sole color
of the January worth it, dry scorched red
like a crimson peppercorn on the mud-dark twig
and think, together, *ocotillo*
in bloom, the same twosome
eked brilliance next to nothing, scarlet fleck
on spider black —
Up lifted.

We see each other
winter through. Beeches
by moonlight / Sagehens in contourline —
chay, chay.
We are bipeds,
we think of two things at a time.

Ruggles' Birthday

for Alan Bernheimer

Rubato: thoughts aloft: Life measured by spent pairs
of shoes with chorus of school girls cracking gum:
Relativity theory thin koolaid compared to St. Francis
conversing with birds.

March 11 reflected in rain-wet street: Damp
bees — fighting over violets? Just a temporary mix-up.
(It is a matter of spiritual thew whose mass is
proto-musical.)

This day / night set-up way too good to last, says
the brass: Man-time above and around worked and
furled like lariat: *trick roping*: rubato! rubato!

Ice melts, but no mail — It's Ruggles' birthday. "He
lived to the ripe age of eighteen sandals." Always a
good word for whinchat or quail.

From Concordia, Kansas

for Robert Harris

The Nazareth Convent 1907
sits above town, settles it
somehow from its hill
the way thought battens time,
fattens the vector.
Around it, grounds
and an aura
of the ample: meadows
where someone's half-through
cutting hay; worn outbuildings;
gardens gone to seed; an orchard
rough around the edges;
dense dark grottoes
of cedars stocked
with statuary and a bench
for contemplation, revelation
of the Galore. Beneath
a grove of elms a range
of fifteen picnic tables,
grove green, wink dappled
on and off by sun. Talk
must be mild there
most of the time: jello salad
with Miracle Whip dressing
reflecting gauzy August sky.
Around it all — it all
interlocks and orbits independently

like a daydream or French chateau —
an ample iron fence
where for a moment I sense boys
kneeling summer dusks,
waiting-in-the-abstract, dawdling
and watching the early lights
come on. (On
their painted ceilings whirls
the Dance of the Bare-naked Nuns.)

Two miles north the river runs,
named after Pawnees,
through late-summer cottonwoods.
A quiet family catfishes
the shady hole below
the highway 81 bridge.
Some of the big trees show
a single yellow leaf
or one small branch of leaves
already molten, golden,
amid the general shimmer: a motif
uncannily repeated
in the restless flocks of redwings
shifting and heaving and tilting
(like loads of grain) with — *zip* —
a single yellowhead mixed in.

On the south side of town
the D. F. Harris Playground Equipment Co.
also sits, a cinder-block shed
in a gravel yard. Around it
a ring of retired merry-go-rounds

and rusty odds and ends
from swing sets lean.
Among the frazzled goldenrod
in one corner a tier
of fancy monkey bars hunkers
like a willow
birds forgot: cold iron pipe twisted
pretzel-wise under coats
of lavender paint: still, still
and left behind in high relief
otherwordly as a common hairpin
happened across on a wild beach.
Orioles stain it from an elm alee.

And that (excepting
the old ten-dollar tourist cabin
by the lake — Humbert Humbert and Lolita
Slept Here) is it
from Concordia — three points
you'll see next time
you're passing through: Air, Water,
and a trace of St. Elmo's Fire
playing along those monkey bars:
The daily given,
the tying of the shoes
this cool clear hard-to-surrender
morning in Concordia, her shapes
and forms unfurled —
Dreamed up, bent, and shipped
by the Delmer F. Harris Co.
around the world.

Satin Street

I.

DETAINER

Mergatroid,
mother of men
whose steel skullplates
pick up radio stations
they hate —

Poor America —

the first broken eggshells
alight in the yard:
Morning birds sing
each other's songs
as men

mothered by Mergatroid
do. Neighbor boy
just dead by burp gun
in Korea, Stalin frothing
in his room, we wet

our hair and comb it
straight up as it dries
into wild electrified roaches
and walk around
like that all afternoon.

2.

YEARS LATER

A nice cold glass of water.
An ice cold glass of water.

My mother a fullblood
I tied notes for no one high
in the lilacs: just the words

there, grapes by night —

sweet-talk satinet equivalent
of leaving pennies on railroad tracks.

Days a Year

APRIL

Dogs have
what kids lost.
Roy has his skull bowl
of cottonwood flowers,
plush crimson and green
(the mother tree bobs
and sways in the wind
like grass in slow
water): food for soft
thought, and I've seen
that mud stuck in *that*
handlebar hole before:
fallen bike, falling bikes,
they go down like dominos
this time of year.
Osier the fearless
puts forth.

MAY

Blocks of May,
chunks of May in blocks
of ice. Strung. Pearlwise.

JUNE

Genus Day-o,
species Halting Vernal,
the dog-eared: low clouds

collar the spruce, soggy grays
clash numbly with fierce new greens.
The apple boughs bow.

"We go out in the night and cut
young onions in the rainy darkness —"
Tu Fu and friend, that we.

We go. We went. We went
and built a *tinga*, then a *mole*,
pouring the cinnamon-chiles

from high above into hot fat.
That was days ago but pockets
of the nose still hang

about the house, low
along the walls and in the shamrocks.
We tap them when we find them,

break them out.

JULY

That new early light in the trees —
familiar face of a stranger, strange
look on the thin friend — it burnishes
the fuselage as all the leaves
show their light sides with something
like a roar: Now here is a sunrise
they will speak of many centuries
down the line.
                        It bronzes the harebells
and basks on a hypersqualid surf-rocked girl
in ersatz leopardskin dress asquat
on random church steps. She is money,
the huge stone wheel sort dragged by bullocks
as seen in Ripley's *Believe It or Not*.

It lights on a harebrain in fine black suit,
expounding. His mouth is open,
his zipper is three-quarters open.
He is change. He passes like a kidney stone.
He knows not the cool of the dirt
three or four inches down.
                        July '49,
the one of a kind: one of my aunts
piles her hair so high and rococo-deco
it snafued Vliet Street traffic in Milwaukee:
High heels struck in syrupy asphalt:
I was tethered nearby
dressed like an organ grinder's monkey,
a roll of caps in my little gun.

Thick July darkening the sky
like many many flocks! Your flies
will be swatted and swept away
with sprigs of marjoram, your tea ceremony
performed on red pinto mules.

AUGUST
rams SEPTEMBER,

the cool nights jar.

OCTOBER

Deciduous man: hot soup:
your bowl has a box elder leaf
in it: your flag shows
purple asters by the bushel,
as in stars,
and the yellow of many schoolbuses
parked beyond a river.

NOVEMBER

Où il se nourrit
Larousse says
regarding the oriole —

the sweet reflexive

flexing, kneading, feeding,
luxuriantly plucking nuts
and berries with both hands
through a pastel cool
like this one —
                    Flash
of mussels marinara
far from here
gleaming in shallows; river
of fish. Eels. Browsing, sifting,
shaking the vines — où *il* means
the world, its traction
and drive.
                    Check the orchards'
pink, gray/pink.
                    Check the pines.

DECEMBER

Little
but a spray of alder
from that sea.

JANUARY

Time vines, time
blossoms —
                    Proviso:
the flicker comes too.

FEBRUARY

Half moon,
half sky: harbingers,
true tidings, light bulbs
above the heads, memoranda
from dream to dream,
thing to thing —
                    dispersed
by wind, spread via bird
droppings or in the cuffs
of ancillary man who
hardly even knows —

standing half a block aroma-
side of the hot chophouse
in brief blue snow.

MARCH

   When the big snows go old dogs stagger from the
houses and re-sniff each inch of pale lawn, pondering
last fall's diluted spoor all morning, scanning the
washed-out leaf wrack, not missing a blade, in a kind
of stiff-legged nirvanic trance —

   Persian patterns, disappearing ink —

   and a hundred particolored crossbills swirl into the
pines along the ridge, still warm from the cornucopia....

97

Elegy 986

Late twentieth century werewolf turbines
rest three minutes a day: glycerin midnight
catwatch and furled cotyledon.
Darrell was swanherd all the way.
Who could care less
for the crap? Barefooted
in hand-tied calf-length cloak
of palmetto fronds: raffia fez: pipe in one
hand, slender willow crook
in the other —
We put that cheese in that tree
because you are dead.

— *Darrell Gray: 1945–1986*

December 16, 1989

1.

Low December candlepower cuts the spruces

2.

Osiers by the tracks in doggo

3.

Until a brief sun riles them oxblood/crimson

4.

Arterial red-of-reds. A stream zigs jet

5.

Through hourold snow: tiny bays of duckweed beam

6.

Bright Spanish olive: hived: city-light-like.

7.

A hem of willows worn basketball orange

8.

Then horses watch, four chestnuts, one gravel gray

9.

From wide field of tall weeds buff and low sienna

10.

Each stalk a tot of snow in the crow's-nest.

11.

Sober alders, lean phragmites

12.

(A word Homer would have known).

13.

The white hills throw a weak pink

14.

Just the color of a redpoll breast.

— *Bozeman, Montana*

Song: Mouth of the Poplar

Slob is dead. I read it
in the *Blat*: Frederick Slob,
58. "The Slobs." But then

they must have said it
with a long, long O: Mr. Slōb
is wearing a robe. Even so ...
Even Wittgenstein ...

And these poplar trees at Poplar
where Poplar River squeezes through
carry their Tinkerbell namesake load
with perfect (mouth-of-Poplar) ease.

— *Poplar, Montana*

July 12, 1990

Anyone once loved
still loved —
              Hollyhocks
open in the alleyways:
                 confectionery
colors: cherry, sweet-tooth pinks,
mallow yellow:
              soda pop colors,
sticky jube jube —
                 But anyone
once loved, still loved.

From the Erstwhile Forks of the Grand

A day gray enough
crickets start to play by noon,
then stop.
         The place
holds its geo-duende
despite the dam's erasure:
her swollen forks
still show
from high points,
their succulent coulees
brightening early this year
trickle from flirtatious
prairie roll to disappear
abruptly, prematurely
into the reservoir
whose waters chop
beneath a heavy-handed autumn
front
skiing in all day on
scathing wind
with just one thing
in mind: Clear the joint,
strip it
like the Khans —
               but
Nothing Personal.

Along the bluffs
we find debris of snake nests
in the sand: signs
of scuffle and four-inch
infant rattlers
curled crisp in death writhe,
cold blooded agony
snuffed by gull or crow
one sunny day —

Where's mama?

I find one crushed flat
in the road, dry
as onionskin, perfect
instant corpus delecti
in mid-stride — blango —
but
   Nothing Personal.
Its tail has a tiny brittle tip
of stuff the color
of thumbnail. I bring it in
for no good reason
and put it in
my Yeats.

A shivering patch
of goldenrod sends
flash of yellow writing
tablets (Goldenrod brand)
from erstwhile Septembers

lost since mossing
and dozing beneath some chilly
backwater bay

and the wind has found
the chokecherry saplings
in a deep ravine
and works them from the top
down: their upper leaves
already burn
with eerie translucent ochre /
rosé
where robins are drunk
on the fruit glut
and visibly hiccoughing

and Sages quake —
man sage, woman sage —
the two species amingle
on the hills,
                balm
to dissipate the notion
that the hideous
is the especially true:
sacred
but not too sacred
but sacred enough
and conveniently rampant,
it is here
to wipe the arse with
as well as cool the heart

with
and clear the mutual air.
Tons of it withing an all-day view
is frankly reassuring,

but it is still August
despite the ashen sky
and all its icing on
the duende and there is
August work to do
from which we will not
be distracted
or blown,
in which we slice the cukes
and Walla Walla sweets
and pile them
in a yellow bowl
to cover with vinegar and water
and a slash
of sugar and set them off
for half a day
to sour up good
and plenty:
                    Done: the 1987 cukes.
The 1987 Forks of the Grand River
coulee cukes.   Done,
and none too soon this blatant
Summer's End
when all things start to stop,
then hurry.

Three Walks

1.

We meet at Jimmy's,
trade grocery bags
of Medicine Bow gooseberries
for day on Sheridan Square.

2.

Did you or did you not
ride a flicker call through it all?

Nocturnal train whistles
are to this continent what
plum blossoms are to Japan.

Were you in Wyoming in 1954?
Did you see Edward Hopper
painting from his car?

3.

Electrologist
with heart of harness leather,
dog iridescent
as a magpie feather.

Allday Purcell

Red church against blue sky, smoke
solfatara from the dreams of whistling
dervish: to escape the danger that the music

will seem to press toward any particular goal.
Starlings hunker at the chimney lip,
pigeons stupid enough to rely solely

on the sun. Brick red,
sky blue, honey for the rods
and cones.   *All ages are contemporaneous*

honey for the bones —
Such that we feijoada in homage.
(Her name in this country would be

Fredericka, but back home
it was "Svedenecka" or "Vredeliecki,"
something of that sort,

nobody really knows
how to pronounce it.)   Such that one morning
we were out at daybreak,

happened across foxes
prancing dalliance in the snow,
also red, also against weak blue sky —

Fox Red, Sky Blue —
Ah Henry
You'll never see seventeenhundred.

Salute: On Peoples Creek

Where it softshoes out
from the inner Bear Paws
and morning glories twine
on the meadow man-sage
I stop this looker noon
to shave — dusty horseface
in the car mirror song sparrows
hum along to.

But it is more than we think:
not Ralph or Cornelius T.
or Orrin U Thant Peoples:
the Atsinas say long ago a wild colt
with human head was born
along this stream. They glimpsed him
now and then, called him *I nit′ ē i:*
"Person," "The Person"
(the English version smudged it,
river jumping track).

Born and reared along this stream,
roamed it all his loversnuts life.

And did those feet
e pluribus unum?
                     Not that we inhabit
a deprived age.

Not that we inhabit
an age at all —
               Switching deerflies
in the goldenrod
with a girlfaced blackbird
on his back.

Penstemon Bearings

1.

The Black Hills lie to in their roads.

Snow on the southern slopes
already melting: "It is late spring,"
writes Charles Chan, "or early summer."

Wind tosses the lilacs generous
in all things, rocks the wasp nest
on its limb, whee-ha.

2.

The Black Hills lie to
in their quarter:

March thirteen
the year's first thunder
broke from their domain:
vernal herald
and ultimatum: Ba-boom
from fifty miles: pedestrians
turn in the streets
caught with their frenchhorns
down! Twenty minutes later
ka-ba-boom
and on through the afternoon:
Patience and vice-grip

of a mud-saint: hatch
of a season —
                    At dusk
a gentle shower danced through town.

                    3.

Your (Hilda Doolittle)
will find Junegrass
skinny in the wind, boney
old grama ablow, and know

what to do: find the track
faint in cool sand
and think *Claro,*
largo, cross White River,

Cottonwood Creek, Hat
and Antelope creeks
with swallows in their shores,
their gaunt millionaire

trees: scan
cut of the bank, layers
stacked for soothsayer,
see grouse go off —

wham — old bones amutter
in pale grass, eyes tearing
with wind, find the round place
where the round stones

stay and cottonwood buds
packed scarlet, dense as roe,
worn Slim Butte far to starboard,
her venerable molar wisdom

with a gap for the chaff to blow
through — *whaff*. You will follow
the draw — Bonnet or Antelope —
trees one by one at your sleeve,

the hawk-dark
deep in the box elder, see
mule deer scat neat in the grass
clean as bird's eggs

and know without asking,
kneel to the tough runt-roses
one hand high (and think
Paris) and from a rise

look far-off at their island
pines and the wind like wheelbirds
in them, and think *Paros* —
that kingfisher sky.

4.

The Black Hills lie to
in their roads —
And "What has love of land
given you? ... And they answered —
Peace."

Today (I see them
from a high window)

they wear a cloudy halo/nimbus,
a simple eastertide atoll.

— *Chadron, Nebraska*

Oriole Diary

Friday: The last time here it was August. We camped among the public lilac bushes and promised to return one spring to see them in bloom.

Now, in latter May, we sit among them — six parallel rows one hundred yards long: lavenders and ivories and purples ten feet tall.

We sit in scented public air and talk about the streamsides thick with wild currant blossom, the sweet yellow blow of the sweet black currants, and vow to come back one fall for the picking.

Saturday: Bloomtime: continuous though staggered aspect of the world: whitecapping to water, poetry amid the general tongue.

Orioles dominate this oasis grove of elms and cottonwoods buffering the lilac plantation from Dakota winds. Their calls and dartings fill the air like the lilacs.

Three hundred years ago this spring, Basho departed on his trajectory through the Far North in search of poetic compounds. Everything within the present 48 hour Sensorium — the billowing trees, the lay of the far hills, this fire of lilac twigs — what they have of English on them is, by poetic tide and instigation, for him.

Sunday: Midday, just after church, a steady trickle of visitors from town, twelve miles north, drive slowly through the grove to see the lilacs: elderly couples, groups of white-haired ladies in floral dresses. Occasionally a car stops on the far side to snitch a mixed bouquet: *Lilac thieves*: a painting (say, Sargent), a daguerreotype, a quick French film.

We sit idling in calm sun and whistle cheap imitations of oriole songs just good enough to bring the males in, bristling and flashing, swooping in overhead to check the stranger with the terrible voice. After two days of their constant comings and goings through the trees, their oranges sizzling, there is a sense of them lacing the air, stitching it with their continuous vectors, wrapping the grove, webbing and fastening the place. (The birds and myself and the Ornithology Club of Osaka see it this way.)

Hot dogs on lilac hot dog sticks: Downwind from smoke and splash and blossom.

— *Forks of Grand River*
South Dakota

Ute Note

What is
that river, does it
have a
name? No.

Interblossom
submontane
Ignacio's

one cool slice
of bunting song —
We take the music
and leave the rind.

He — a Ute
with foresight —
says Goodbye,
I will
see you again
some time.

Song

Remember
the marsh arabs,
reed canoes
through Euphrates
marshlands:

Living on fish,
reed houses afloat
on baled-reed islands:
Water people,

skew-o-morph:
cries of terns
sharp
through the headlands.

Two Walks

I.

Dreamt
I was driving
a sixties Mustang
bearing on Chicago

pure and simple
through roan March sky,
crow flocks skirting
the woodlots,

thinking of dinner
that night with Johnny —
Rumanian oxtails
and gypsy fiddle —

looking forward
to the borzoi faces
of Baltic women
on the downtown streets,

cheekbones riding high:
hallmark, blazon
and refrain of that city
in my comicbook

of hours —
I watch for them
from the Greyhound
and down off the trains.

2.

Madame '87:
her potent Fall:
something tenor, something
mimbreño to it

I think of
here in December,
almost hear.

Song: Forks of the Smoky Hill

Season through place,
Place in season, in place:
   crux of it, *cruz*:
   cave of the heart
      weevil:

Why me, hackberry —
I am your friend. One song
per season. Throw of
yucca seeds lacquer black
   comes up

Cool wonder of
All lives: one song per:
Zebra swallowtail
   touch down,
   confer.

Piss Ant and Peony

The word *peony*
like the word *firefly*
held so powerful a charge
for the Japanese
it was used in poems
sparingly, with great care

and Harry
was Thomas Eakins'
dog. He watched
the Philadelphia fireflies
from his stoop. His master
brought home one night
a new painting called
"Whistling for Plover."

Harry watched the dandelion
fluff
drift by with constant
wonder.   (It slows
but never stops —

Whistling for plover.
Whistling for lover.
Whistling for peony —
Peony.

Mouth of the Whosis

for Ted Berrigan

I.

THE CANNONBALL AT CANNON BALL

That week's stars the brightest I remember except for a few in the bassinet. Suspiciously bright — enough to make you buy a paper to see what's going on. All the famosas. Then a slender new one coming on off Taurus: Phalange, the Finger.

At Bismarck (far from the Cannonball) there was a quarter moon of thumbnail on the café table below a dirty plastic rose. It looked friendly and old. Dressed differently, bedded on velvet in a 2 inch cypress box with sliding stained glass top, it might have brought thousands at Sotheby's relic auction.

> Dear Johnny B.,
> these compositions are by
> none other than
> Alessandro Scarlatti
> and I desire you to tell no one
> that things of the greatest worth
> are concerned.

2.

THE RED BELOW CLARENCE

The red a break from the water color blue: carburetor function of *Otherwise* in everyday life: those whole other tracks with a whole other city waiting all dressed up at the end: Just pre-dusk and the stadiums lit. Dancers are dressing and undressing. By the robin's tone you know the very tree. From good friends upwind wafts of basswood flower and bacon grease — sharp, word-like....

Falsetto Tarzan yells from across the river. A low roar of bees.

3.

THE KANAWHA AT NITRO

Ka-now, they say it, and its coolwawa valley happens to be ablaze with October color — mauve, gamboge, sienna: Wall of fruitage with a man-shaped hole in it. *He just left....*

Ka-now, the terminal vowel seeping back through underground channels to leaven the middle *a*.

*

Little Leon (pop. 50) was easy.

Black Betsy was easy: trusty white houses dovetailed in above the tracks: Many beeskins.

Pliny, almost nonexistent on the other shore, was ready when we got there. It has the broad workable side of the valley and doesn't need a thing.

But Nitro was impossible.

We tried looking not quite at it, rather, off to one side the way they handle difficult stars.

We re-did it from the ground up with a tiny secret law à la Navajo blanket weavers, not to tempt the perfectionist.

We rebuilt it as grandma's own cherry pie with a single pit left in the timber for luck and good company, and not to tempt the perfectionist.

Roy slipped down near the river below town and chose a small, sunny locust tree he approached as a stand-up bass and caressed a few times with his fiddle bow.

Nothing worked for Nitro.

It lacks the beatific node.

4.

THE CANADIAN WITH THE ANTELOPE HILLS

Tengri, "Eternal Blue Sky," Sir: beloved of prairie drivers: Thin Air. Christ, the botanical, Comanche in the rain. Big Gypsy, the traceless, *gypto americanus* who descended on the town odd summers: every boy on his bike to the outskirts to see them at the laundromat before the sheriff showed them to the county line. On the car top cheap pine stencils flapped and chafed, for hire to slap down hopscotch grids in yellow paint on playgrounds. Illinois plates.One moonless night they pilfered all the roses: poof.

Horse breaker, dog eater, chicken thief. Honey dipper, burlap mender, stewer of over-the-hill tripe. Creel weaver, loon skinner, fence cutter. Bone crusher, latrine digger, egg sucker. Feather peddler wearing an ear of field corn down in the pants to impress the ladies: Big party at 36N/100W: "Rock Breaks Scissors."

5.
THE ARIKAREE AT COPE

Waxwings, bells — the little round ones girls wore on their shoes in high school — for Best of Class, say, mid-November: cool wandering willows Chicago-to-LA pilots dip to see.

★

Simone knows a sideroad with cortege from town: three on a side, guitar or two trailing, hauling an old bathtub with legs and a hole in it to chuck over the bridge. (Throbbing bass line.) And where coyotes rolled that jumped a fence and ate computer chips.

"Sane as sunshine," they say in the South.

Size 9.

Size 9.

6.

THE TRUCKEE AT RENO

Jules Verne clouds above the mountains show an arm
— the one strong arm of a polenta chef — and hold
snow. "Corn snow" probably. This is France: leather
jackets out for the first time, the Pistil and Stamen statue
above tame ducks. If you're up early enough you'll see
spitoon cleaners wander in to shop the stalls for bunches
of scouring rush. This is hawksbeard, wahoo, buggywhip
maple. This is Swaziland: the month-dead emperor
Sobhuza II sits in a high secret cave wrapped in freshly
slaughtered bull skins. I wonder did they sew them up to
shrink as rawhide to form an armored capsule, or what.
Pour bees or honey in? Cold water: Snow, slow boiling
in those clouds for hours. Glen's Face. Harry's Eyes. The
naming as opposed to the sending of the flowers.

7.

MESA VERDE 2

Moments it was any German oompah restaurant with
ravens.

*

Sunday mornings early on a tinge of perking coffee
drifted from the kitchen up and through a medium elm,
around a corner to my window. Followed shortly by a
hint of blueberry muffins. Fifteen minutes later, bacon
twitching in the pan. About noon a baking apple pie

seeped up, clipped by the ozone of a short-lived rain.

Lower away the little basket on a string.

Then the boy upstairs raps his pipe on the folklorico
ashtray and the woman in her eighties next door sits
down at the piano for her daily romp through Chopin
— I hear the bench scrape on a hardwood floor. On the
right day come Octobers she ventures down to the lawn,
builds a tiny elm leaf fire and flips an unlit Camel in,
then moves back to the swing downwind and (ankles
together, hands folded) graciously sucks it in like pearly
incense or belladonna. Homage to an ancient Viennese
Fall I think — she studied music in her twenties there:
Pictures on her wall.

Hanging it like meat. Merry and light as at a Fuji-
viewing party.

Then a steady pork roast through the afternoon.

*

It was gusting you and Lower East Side.

It's still a perfect place to spawn.

It was tracking down a legendary Mississippi blues
man unheard of since the '30s and finding him one
morning, just washing up his breakfast dishes on the
edge of town, still 29.

8.

THE MEDICINE BOW ON ITS OWN NORTH OF HANNA

Thus the mallard whipping down the Mississippi hears
surf awash on *both* coasts;
And early Egyptian muslims retained a pre-Islam holi-
day, a spring one with mandatory meal in the countryside
— (Infraction punishable by tweezing of the compleat
hair?);
And sage be wealth and gravy, the *a capella* flats hung
thigh-high, blue with valence, poised like bonsai planta-
tions, scenting the air —
Johnny B. Appleseed, Johnny B. Myrrh:
Small
choirs for the sage hymn and for the hands and knees
an understory starred with cushion phlox and miles of
pastel lichens, set, clean as gingham near the sea.
Thus the mudballs stacked for drying.

Roll out barrels
of pickled beets
with eggs, stand them up
along the roads — float dollops
of ricotta in —
that the tongues be red
and big herons lift from the shores.

9.

THE REPUBLICAN NEAR MAX

In one of those fields of plum-colored grasses a man
was there with his back to the river and his hands in his
pockets, apparently watching the train go by. He wore
his pants low and was saying something for as long as I
could twist around in the seat to see: something steady
and clear-cut and mild: a lip-reader's meat, but there was
none.

For the 10 thousandth time I think, Someday I'll meet
someone from this little burg or that crossroads and say
"I was through there on the train once" and mention the
hulk of a hotel gathering moss near the station, or the
brilliant landmark mass of bittersweet on a fencerow at
the edge of town.

His words hang unwasted, hold formation, scale in
a bevy downvalley just above the rusty willows and the
river ripe with messages in corked vials (an old one of
mine for Kansas still kicking — hope it makes it through
the dam), veer along that hacksaw ridge, through a floppy
pack of crows, and up into the vedas, the agrapha and
jive, *huh*'s and sleeptalk, stupid questions, wrong direc-
tions, goodbyes at the stations, over slang slicks, past the
Cellini cluster (the well-oiled flurry in a dark alley that
paralyzed thieves), suitcases and silos full, hocus pocus,
mumbo jumbo stirring gravel in kames, burps after pas-
senger pigeon, sounds only Mavis Staples makes, last
words, casual dismissals, calling dogs, summing ups (*the
hairball got 'em*) ...

And down again sooner or later maybe right about here
on the volatile North Fork, planing in to close the circuit.

Flyspecks to this point, when they reach our friend
again he'll jump up, click his heels, zoom away over the
hills like Farmer Alfalfa —

Poeticized.

Goosed into song.

10.

THE BIG BLUE AT THE EDGE OF CRETE

Maples flame beside the Museum of the Tramp:
a mean wind through its chicken-wire windows, but
the ashes are the cool bowls of fire this year, ashimmer
with high *pococurante*: peach and melon tones, russets and
rose, cinnamons, flicker eye with curry dream, and some-
thing almost *melon-rind*. All verging, all lit from within,
again.

*

Old men discuss on the bank, a hand-drawn map as
white of the eye: Just cool enough to spend their days
collecting buckets of sheep chips in the pastures for fuel
— young men get all the cow dung — or combing river
bottoms, briar patches, for rabbit and white-tail pellets.
(These burn with a Low Wild Flame: *size 3, size 3.*)

THE MISSISSIPPI AT BURLINGTON

You get three and a half minutes as the train curls
around it between the station and the bridge: a giant
tired grain elevator complex beside the river: four huge
silos like organ pipes connected by a chute to a blank box
building the size of Notre Dame with a three story some-
thing perched on top: cocky gray, curiously trim for 500
feet up: sloping roofs and dormer windows catching the
sun: Asking for it —

A hotel, one of these days.

A smoky dining room waiters hurry through with arms
full of ironweed and sunflowers.

Some folks stop for catfish in season; some for the stee-
ples, or the chili. You can buy live fritillaries at the desk.

There was a homesick girl from the Georgia moun-
tains staying in one of the garrets, working her way back
east. Every first her mother mailed a homemade fruitcake
— brown wrapping, white string — and she would show
up that evening in the lobby, going from person to person
passing out paper-thin slices with a tear in one eye.

A. S. Hitchcock crossed the final *t* in his monumental
Manual of the Grasses of the United States in room 99.

A high open terrace overlooks the landing, a major
Midwest drop-off for circus gear and animals. There was
usually at least one small outfit or carnival bivouacked
along shore, summers, waiting for a young elephant or a
spare Percheron to arrive by barge.

We got to know a midway weight-guesser who took his
evening cigar to the hotel pier, just within hailing distance

of the elderberry wine vendors. He had worked much of the known world and was fluent in pounds, kilos, founts, arrobas, catties, and stones.

He loved those two or three day breaks from his constant attune to human gravity — he called it the Glue — he took his work seriously — but August nights when townspeople and hotel guests cruised the embarcadero looking for a breeze he couldn't help snapping off a quick figure for a sun-burnt Ichabod Crane type or a pregnant woman —

"Mother 127, child 5½."

He wore red paper shoes, grilled 14¾ ounce steaks on a shovel, and took his bedtime whiskey high in the Burlington Grand — which never existed, never might — and yet it was somehow included.